Suffering for Christ

By Chelsea Kong

Just to say thanks for downloading my book, I would like to give you the audio book version 100% free.

Email: kayunkk@gmail.com

Printed in 2021-2022, Made in Toronto, Canada
ISBN: 978-1-990399-17-6
Legal Deposit, Library and Archives Canada

Dedicated to the Lord for His glory

The Lord has proven that He is well able to provide for us and cares about us. We learn to listen and to keep a distance or to cut ties with people who are not beneficial to our lives. Value those who genuinely care and help you.

Contents

Introduction

The Lord Jesus Christ told us that we will suffer persecution for His name. Our world has already begun to have a division between Christians and non-Christians. Among the believers, we have those who are fully serving the Lord and following the Holy Spirit versus those who are a type of Christian but not led by the Holy Spirit. When we suffer for the Lord, the greater the honor we bring to our Lord. We must truly die to the flesh and live for Christ. Then the beauty of the Lord will be revealed from within us and be shown outwardly.

John 12:24
"Very truly I tell you, unless a kernel of wheat falls to the ground and dies, it remains only a single seed. But if it dies, it produces many seeds."

We live in a world where people are afraid of a virus and once somebody gets sick they call it covid. Test kits and hospital tests are used. Flu and cold appear to sign similar to covid. During this time, it's winter and more people are afraid of the virus spreading and rushing to get vaccinated for the first time. There has become a shortage of the Pzifer vaccine and now they only have Moderna until they get more. Pharmacies have waitlists of people waiting to be vaccinated. Most people seeking to get Pzifer and at the same time the government mandates the booster shot as a requirement. Some news later is discussing the fourth. It seems that it is endless as variants are happening. There is a question with two views concerning this.

Unvaccinated are being labeled and separated from the vaccinated. The complication of not being fully vaccinated is become another threat. We are in a world where rich people are in control. We are forced to have to obey the government or suffer out on certain enjoyment. Control has been set in place that we can't travel freely without proof of vaccination. Only those who have a vehicle can still travel within the country's boundaries. Those without have to sacrifice traveling if they don't follow the rules. In the days to come, people will get arrested if they seek to escape and haven't complied with the Anti-Christ system.

The doctor will advise you to get vaccinated once you have recovered. They don't have to physically check you, but just speak to you on the phone or virtually to prescribe what you should do. There is so much fear and uncertainty. People are forced to isolate themselves to control the virus and disinfectants are used to kill any traces that may spread.

Chapter 1: Sufferings in time of sickness

A lady is suffering without a job and has to move out end of the month. The job requires double vaccination to keep it. The fear of DNA alteration prevents one from wanting to take a risk. At the same time, it is great suffering and loss. A good job becomes more difficult to get when there is a mandatory requirement involved. The concern for finances becomes stressful especially when you are told that you may not qualify for Employment Insurance. If you got terminated from your job because you didn't comply, then you may face great difficulty finding another job. Two months without income. This is a test of faith for provision after such a decision is made. We may think that our friends are speaking on behalf of the Lord, but we need to test what they tell us. People can speak things out of care and concern, but it can be the enemy's way to deter us from obeying the Lord and cause us to suffer loss. It is so easy to blame others when that happens. We need to hear God now and, in the days, to come. One mistake and our lives are at risk and you don't know when you will come out of your situation.

Can you handle the pressure of having bills, rent, and the need for food to eat? Those without a family to support them find it the most difficult challenge to handle. This is when we need to use all our wisdom and pray for the Lord to guide us on what to do. How long can you endure? Do you have friends and a church willing to support you? If everyone is against you, how will you handle it?

Your employer tells you that you can apply for work again after you comply with the mandatory vaccine policy, but you will be considered a new hire and lose all the seniority that you gained previously. You knew that you qualified for a permanent job had you not been terminated. You were so looking forward to your job promotion but didn't succeed at the interview. You feel disappointment and yet there is hope for you though it's not going to be the same as before. Your efforts before are wasted just because of this one bad decision. Your mind tells that if you listened to the Lord this would not have happened. We need to discern those we consider our friends. The enemy may use our friends to deceive us. discern those we consider our friends. The enemy may use our friends to deceive us.

In a time of isolation for 10 days, one lady suffered. She was forced to have to pay for Tylenol Complete medication to take to deal with the virus and a spray of disinfectant. She is told to open the window to make sure that the virus leaves and questioned if she has any symptoms after a few days. Another test is required to ensure that there is no virus. She is required to spray the disinfectant from above and to the ground in the washroom before entering, exiting, the hallway, and until her bedroom door.

She is not able to go out to get food to eat and cannot have food to cook. The kitchen is off-limits. Food was given to me a few items at a time and chosen for her. At first, there is only one meal a day. Then two meals. This is a time when fasting and praying are forced on a person. She had only one meal a day in the evening to eat while in isolation for the first few days. It is the most challenging time. She was fortunate to have some snacks, dried and canned goods that she had stored in case of emergencies. In the time of quarantine, good food is required for one to recover. One must have lots of fluids, especially water and soup.

She felt the pangs of hunger come upon her waiting for a meal to eat. She isn't given any choice in what she is allowed to eat. Certain foods were requested, but she was given what was chosen for her to eat. Some fruits, pasta, rice, soup, fish, chicken, and vegetables are some of the food selections. Other food had to be provided by friends and other believers. This is when having friends and those in Christ makes a huge difference. The food had to be delivered directly to the residence door for the roommate/landowner to pick up to give to the isolated lady. She is at the mercy of the roommate/landowner and forced to cooperate to keep the peace.

Hard lessons are learned when we don't follow the instruction of the Lord and when we hear too many counselors giving us advice whether it's friends or a pastor. We need to consult the Lord directly about what He wants us to do. Not everyone who speaks to us is giving us a word from the Lord or counsel that applies to our situation, so we must have the discernment to recognize God's voice. He speaks in quietness. Every decision we make determines the direction and events to happen. The Lord will bring us out of trouble. Punishment happens when we don't heed instructions. People may call you rebellious and coming against authority.

Daniel consulted the Lord and then found favour and with wisdom from the Lord, He asked to be fed water and vegetables. He requested to be tested for 10 days eating only these. Fasting and prayer brought wisdom, knowledge, understanding, and the interpretation of dreams to Daniel's life. When we make mistakes, people will scold us and others may abandon us. We get chastised and the devil is glad that we are suffering. We get corrected and taught a heavy lesson for the decisions we make. We may get ridiculed and put to shame. Others may despise us. The Lord is still with us even in these times. It is better to suffer for righteousness than for doing wrong.

The lady is emotionally disturbed and found it difficult to pray, worship, and seek the Lord as she feels sad. For one who is not so strong to endure, it is easier to become emotional and swayed in your faith. Loneliness and tears of despair. She thinks about how she made mistakes and feels the emotional pain of the choices. She is feeling anger for the counsel of friends advising her that it is better not to take the vaccine and lose her job and find another one. DNA alteration is not worth you keeping the job. God will provide for you. Trust Him and that you can get another job even a minimum wage job. That is not what she wants and it may be the only kind of job available. You must have faith in God. People scold her that she doesn't have enough faith because she wants to give in to comply to get a job. This is also how the devil can use people to speak words to provoke you if God has not told you not to comply. The pressure builds over time. She feels the tension and stress. She gets worried about how she is going to pay rent, etc. She has to find a new place where they don't require or allow her time. She looks for work. For two months, there are no responses. The tension builds and she looks and applies for whatever government benefits she can get, which isn't much. She takes a chance to apply for EI praying she will get it though they have mentioned before that they might not pay people who have been terminated for not complying with the mandate.

She prays to the Lord and cries out to Him. She feels lonely and suffering until she can speak with other believers who can pray and fellowship with her to encourage and support her. She felt helpless in her situation. Too many people had advised her what they believe the Lord is telling her to do. She felt frustrated and angry. She is scared and not confident. Sometimes the family may not understand. It's most difficult when your family doesn't fully support what you believe. We are accountable to the Lord for our actions.

The lady also must wait for her ordered food to be delivered to her door to eat and she can't go to the front door to get her food. She must wait for the landowner/roommate to answer her phone call and go to get the food from the front door. It could be hours before she can have the food. The Lord is gracious to grant us our request when He knows we need it. He is faithful to provide for all our needs and more than what we need. The lady who was suffering hunger and persecution recovered. The enemy can stir up further difficulties even when we are overcoming our struggles.

The one the devil was stirring up began to take control insisting that she contact her doctor to find out what to do. The next day she also pushed her to call public health because the rapid test she required her to take showed positive.

The receptionist gave the public health phone number to ask for general information. The phone line says that she just needs to isolate herself for 10 days. She had been taking Tylenol Complete from a 40 pack that was purchased for her. When she called the Public Health line again to speak to a nurse she was told that she is no longer contagious and there is not much cough. She can get the vaccine as required by the doctor. It is normal for people to still have a slight lingering cough.

A week more will help the cough go, but she can speak to the City Public Health line to ask. The rapid test will show positive for a month because of the residue in the body, but the virus is no longer contagious after 10 days of isolation. Anyone who has had the virus three months ago cannot cause somebody to be infected by it.

The one the enemy has used refused to accept this information and insisted that the lady must get a PCR test to prove she is negative. She assumed she is not well and that she must clean with soap and water everything she touches. She accused her that she feels cold chills after the lady had gotten vaccination. Also, she told her that she should go out because she is not well. Though, at the same time, she is driving her to move out. and didn't want to allow her to stay any longer past the end of February. She wants her to find a new place. How can she find a new place if she cannot go outside to check?

She is already not sick and even others had confirmed this. She faced a Pharaoh type like Moses faced Pharoah. She overcome and did what she needed to do according to her schedule and needs. She only felt a bit of tiredness and some difficulty due to the snowy weather that caused a great amount of snow to fall. It made it a challenge to walk as the sidewalks had not been cleared up.

The scripture tells us in 2 Corinthians 4:8-10 - We are troubled on every side, yet not distressed; we are perplexed, but not in despair;

We became disappointed and our faith is tested. Can you endure not having a job and having to move out? How about little food to eat also? The Lord Jesus Christ suffered at the hands of man being beaten and bruised. He warned us that we will be persecuted in the last few days. Even our family members will turn on us. How about believers? The enemy can use the people we live us against us. It becomes our test. Do you have the fruit of the Holy Spirit? Are you baptized and led by the Holy Spirit?

The enemy will test your faith to make you prove who you are in Christ. This is the real test of your character in Christ. The Lord wants us to be His representative. When others can't see who you are in Christ, they will treat you indifferently. This is where conflicts and division happen. They will treat you in the flesh especially when the individual who you are dealing with is not the same type of Christian as you are. If they cannot see the fruit and character of Christ in you, they will begin to teach and test you. The devil will use this to create hardship and persecution. He will make it so difficult for both of you to get along that division happens. You only get so many chances to improve the situation. The roommate/landowner will seek to throw you out of their home once they reached their limit. There is much stress involved.

1 Peter 3:17 ESV
For it is better to suffer for doing good if that should be God's will, than for doing evil.

There is punishment also that will happen for one who evicts a true believer and does harm or mistreatment. We must also be careful when we provoke others to anger. Not all sufferings we face are for Christ. Serving Christ includes the ministry of intercession and spiritual warfare. The devil hates it when we wage war against his kingdom and destroy his works. We have the authority in Christ against them. We must be careful also when he uses situations to attack us like taking away our job, getting us kicked out of a home, and making us suffer hunger.

Families and relatives have been persecuting one another in certain countries, but during this pandemic, even those without the vaccine are being persecuted by their family and friends. The threat and fear have caused this. Jesus warned us it will happen and it will be more in the coming years. We already see that within the household even between a landowner, roommates, and tenants God's love can grow cold. People become less willing to forgive each other. One can also suffer from beingmisunderstood. The Lord heals us from our brokenness so that the devil cannot use anything to bring division. Rebellion before the Lord is equal to witchcraft.

Luke 12:53
The father shall be divided against the son, and the son against the father; the mother against the daughter, and the daughter against the mother; the mother in law against her daughter in law, and the daughter in law against her mother in law.

Chapter 2: External Persecutions

In the days to come, the Internet and electricity will be lost if you don't have the mark of the beast. We will not be able to use anything we currently have. We have to go into survival mode like how it was in the past. Mennonites and others that still use the old method of living are more prepared. They have already learned how to live life without modern technology. The Lord gives us wisdom on how to prepare for days ahead when we ask Him.

Everything is controlled and monitored from outside the room where she must remain. She was not able to leave her room, but only to go washroom and take a shower. The roommate/landowner messaged and called to check on the lady whenever she needed to communicate with her. This is a model of how the Anti-Christ soldier deals with those who will refuse the mark of the beast. If there is no co-operation, punishment will be invoked and suffering. The one the enemy uses may not always be merciful. In this case, she didn't want to have to cook or reheat food for the lady in isolation. She didn't fully concern if she can afford to buy takeout food to eat. She is scared about the virus and scared that she won't get rent money. She even requested somebody to come to the unit and take the isolated lady away. During quarantine, you cannot travel anywhere and it's the only way the virus can be controlled from spreading. She still has access to communicate with others.

We tend to forget that we are in spiritual warfare even when we deal with people every day. The enemy doesn't want us to be in unity and peace. We must take authority over every thought that comes to mind. We have been given the authority to change our situation and everything in life to line up with God's will. Know who you are in Christ and the authority that He has given. Exercise that authority. The devil will be against you, but Christ is with you. He will seek to make you doubt and put all kinds of thoughts in your mind to shake your faith. He will make the circumstances difficult and bring confu

sion. He will cause you to be in conflict and strife in your relationships.

Ephesians 6:12
12 For we wrestle not against flesh and blood, but principalities,
against powers, against the rulers of the darkness of this world,
against spiritual wickedness in high places.

2 Corinthians 1:5
Casting down imaginations, and every high thing that exalteth itself against the knowledge of God, and bringing into captivity every
thought to the obedience of Christ;

The Anti-Christ is very controlling and uses companies to moni-
tor all our online and offline activities. Churches are being forced to
go online and use Zoom and Facebook where they can be tracked.
Nothing is private anymore in our generation. Due to the vaccine
passports, it tracks more details about us. Eventually, the Anti-Christ
system will have all our information onto a chip system. They will
know everything about us and where we go. Our emails, chats, texts,
calls, video calls, social media, etc are all monitored. Everything we
post is recorded. There are only a few that respect our privacy and
will maintain that. Sometimes people are scared to use technology
due to a lack of safety. Our phone is an ID that tracks all our activities. GPS will easily allow people to locate you. One day, you may
travel somewhere and the enemy will be able to locate you. We have
heard of stalkers. Satellite technology and tracking apps make it easy
for tracking anyone. They just need your name, cell phone, or license
plate.

Creditors can easily find information about you on the Internet and
call your work number. They can find out your home phone number
and address. It is much easier with a 5G network integrated into a
chip system especially injected or tattooed into the human body to be
easily tracked. Be aware that it's coming. We've been warned that ID
cards will become useless.

The unvaccinated already are not allowed to travel anywhere. The unvaccinated are being isolated and charged additional fees. There is division and segregation. People are being forced to have booster shots as additional protection. One day we won't be able to leave the city we are in. We have been warned that military law is coming. Once it does, nobody will have freedom. When the military takes over, they will not show mercy. The Jews suffered under the hands of Hitler. It will be worse when the Anti-Christ is in charge. All the kings of the earth will grant him the authority and power to rule over the nations. Man will seek to protect themselves rather than one another.

Revelation 17:13
These have one mind and shall give their power and strength unto the beast.

When the Anti-Christ has set up his government system, which is linked through the mark that he will set up, many will suffer these things and maybe more. If you take the mark, then you will be able to buy, sell, and do everything supposedly that you normally did, but it will cost your soul for eternity. If you choose not to take it, you will suffer persecution, punishment, and death. You will have no income, job, home, etc. Everything will be taken from you because you won't be able to afford to pay for anything. You will be in debt and unable to buy food and basic needs. People will either seek to survive or they will perish.

A foretaste of what is coming is that people already decided not to get the covid-19 vaccine and those who refused lost their job and companies start to demand double vaccination. Not everyone has the faith or favour to have a job without being vaccinated. Yes, there are remote jobs out there, but the Lord is the one who gives us the job. He decided for each one what we must do. Those who manage to find a job that doesn't require it can spare themselves, but others when they consult the Lord for guidance have been directed to take the vaccine and believe Him that they will be protected. They keep

keep their job. Some have to suffer a bit of time before they receive a job where they aren't forced to get vaccinated, but others are forced to decide to get it since they couldn't get work or have a place to live if they don't. Search the scriptures to see if there is anything that speaks against vaccinations. Find out what the Word says. So, far there is no actual scripture that tells us this.

Believers are to trust the Lord in a time of the pandemic to hold onto the Word of God more tightly. We have such passages as Psalm 91 and Ephesians 6:10-18. Our protection against anything that the enemy sends our way. The Blood of Jesus has the power to destroy every sickness and disease. The Blood of Jesus conquers all things.

Revelation 12:11
And they have conquered him by the blood of the Lamb and by the word of their testimony, for they loved not their lives even unto death.

The Lord made our DNA and has the power to protect it. When we received Him, we were given Jesus' eternal life that has the power to save and protect. It has everything that we need. The Lord tells us to trust Him. He has the power to save even those who have taken the vaccine. This has been proven as we lead one to Christ even shown in a vision it can happen. The Lord is not a man that He would lie to. In the days ahead, the mark will be the seal that will cause a man to lose his soul. That is what the scripture says. We must know where is the mark. It says clearly the forehead and forearm or right hand and not any other part of the body.

Revelation 13:16-18 KJV
And he causeth all, both small and great, rich and poor, free and bond, to receive a mark in their right hand, or their foreheads: And that no man might buy or sell, save he that had the mark, or the name of the beast, or the number of his name. Here is wisdom. Let him that hath understanding count the number of the beast: for it is the number of a man, and his number is Six hundred threescore and six.

Believers will be tested for their faith in the Lord. We are only at the beginning of that testing. We are not yet in severe suffering. Our faith is being tested if we trust the Lord to provide for us in such a time as this. We need great wisdom to survive the coming sufferings. People who have gathered and planned well may have a better chance for what is coming, but still, they are not in control of the future. When currency begins to fail, it will become useless. People say that we must prepare. This global pandemic has already caused shortages and people to panic. We become at the mercy of the authorities to give us government assistance in these times for those who have lost their job or have suffered in their business.

Those who suffer for Christ will have great rewards in heaven. There are scriptures to tell us to also look to the Lord when we go through tribulations, trials, etc.

Romans 5:3-5
And not only so, but we glory in tribulations also: knowing that tribulation worketh patience; And patience, experience; and experience, hope: And hope maketh not ashamed; because the love of God is shed abroad in our hearts by the Holy Ghost which is given unto us.

1 Peter 5:10 - But the God of all grace, who hath called us unto his eternal glory by Christ Jesus, after that ye have suffered a while, make you perfect, establish, strengthen, settle you.

James 1:2-4 - My brethren, count it all joy when ye fall into divers temptations;
1 Peter 4:12-19 - Beloved, think it not strange concerning the fiery trial which is to try you, as though some strange thing happened unto you:
John 16:33 - These things I have spoken unto you, that in me ye might have peace. In the world ye shall have tribulation: but be of good cheer; I have overcome the world.

Remember, there will be those in Christ that will perish as martyrs for their faith. You may have seen some movies talking about the tribulation where the believers either took the mark or they decided to die for their faith. We are coming closer to that time. The world is changing faster than we planned. Believers are being warned to prepare for famines and greater difficulties.

2 Timothy 3:1-5 ESV
But understand this, that in the last days there will come times of difficulty. For people will be lovers of self, lovers of money, proud, arrogant, abusive, disobedient to their parents, ungrateful, unholy, heartless, unappeasable, slanderous, without self-control, brutal, not loving good, treacherous, reckless, swollen with conceit, lovers of pleasure rather than lovers of God, having the appearance of godliness, but denying its power. Avoid such people.

Chapter 3: Suffering under authority

There are times of suffering under those placed in authority over us. A boss may reduce an employee's hours because of seeing failure in performance and eventually they will not schedule the employee for work. In some cases, they may only assign a few hours of work. They control when the person should be scheduled. They may be harsh and seek to teach the employee a lesson. They assign them to do tasks that they don't enjoy to maintain the success of the store. It feels degrading or disrespectful. They may question your beliefs if they believe they are Christian and know that you are, but don't see your attitude reflects it. God knows who you are, but not everyone else sees it. You may get judged out of the nature of your flesh. You find it difficult to represent Christ before that person because they attack certain highly sensitive areas. It is easy sometimes to get offended. Think about how much more people will become offended in the days to come. If we cannot forgive now, it will be more difficult later. Some have honored Christ and suffered at the hands of evil people, but their suffering is not as severe as those in the Bible that we read. Each one must take up their cross and suffer for Christ. Do God's will with the expectation that you will be persecuted. Remember that not everyone will support you, but the Lord is with you. He will fight for you. He will comfort you and He can send the right people into your life to be there for you in your difficulty. There is a time frame that you need to wait before the victory comes. God is always on time. He has His perfect time for everything. Our flesh needs to die out before we can inherit the blessings. It requires much patience to wait for the Lord's deliverance. It is so easy for us to forget and worry. God is still in control. He will deal with our enemies.

1 Timothy 6:12 KJV
"Fight the good fight of faith, lay hold on eternal life, whereunto thou art also called, and hast professed a good profession before many witnesses."

2 Timothy 4:7-8 KJV
I have fought a good fight, I have finished my course, I have kept the faith: Henceforth there is laid up for me a crown of righteousness, which the Lord, the righteous judge, shall give me at that day: and not to me only, but unto all them also that love his appearing.
We need to stay strong and thankful.

1 Thessalonians 5:18
give thanks in all circumstances; for this is God's will for you in Christ Jesus.

There is a time when a lady worked at a Hallmark store and the manager there was determined to generate profit at the store. If you were to visit Fairview Mall, you would find out that the store is gone. It was closed down a year or so after she quit the job. The manager pushed sales and because she wanted to improve the sales in the store she put the best workers who could drive sales at the cash. Anyone else she placed around the store to help the customers or promote the products. She insisted that this staff promotes a push button toy when they purchase three cards they would get it at a discount. She made her stand at the front of the store to show and promote to the customers that came in. She made sure that she didn't come to the cash. She was standing and monitoring. One of the staff would purposely sign her name in the cash registers to get the sales and other colleagues that are her friends didn't mind and helped her too. She also was very good at upselling to clients to get them to purchase more products. People would buy from her. At the end of the day, the lady was forced to promote at the front of the door and had to also vacuum while the rest of the colleagues counted the cash. The manager even had to arrange a schedule to make sure every staff took turns vacuuming the store. It seemed that this lady was always stuck doing it each shift that she worked instead of just doing it once a week. The manager was not very fair to her also. She also limited her work hours and didn't grant her the days off she wanted on certain holidays. She had to write a note to tell the manager she is not available instead of saying please and thank you.

This manager was bullying her. She questioned her about her beliefs and said "Do you not pray?" The lady responded that she does. This manager is of a different type of Christianity and didn't understand. Her attitude reflected what she knew. We don't always see the results we desire nor do we understand. The manager favoured the non-Christian and then the others. She even recommended and made her an assistant manager to manager level of the Hallmark Outlet store for the duration that it was open. It happened there was also another believer that was persecuted by this main manager and she eventually quit the job before this lady did.

The Lord later revealed that this was a persecution situation and that she successfully overcame that and moved on to a better job. Her life also changed but she had to go through further tests with other bosses before she could get the best job and better accommodation. She also gained new friends but also went through other difficulties in life. She learned she cannot trust people but it took her time to discern people's hearts.

Teachers also had bullied her before when she was in college. She went through a bad experience with a teacher that considered a bad person. She lacked the necessary instinct required to recognize the children's needs from a broader classroom perspective. The teacher was feeling concerned for the children but judging and incriminating her that she is making the children suffer or something. The reality is that she didn't know how to apply the theory that she learned from Early Childhood Education into the classroom on a practical level when dealing with children. She thought she was doing that but in the teacher's eyes, she was just observing the children and talking. The dean of the program spoke to her and told her that she should find another program to study and that she is not capable to interact with the children. This devastated her.

Besides, the job she also was persecuted in the home by various owners in different scenarios.

Chapter 4: Persecution in the home

Some people know how to get their friends to help them and know how to make them like them. Others have to deal with things mainly alone because people find them to be needy or they heard some lie and decided not to support them. Those who try not to rely on friends, but on the Lord face challenges in life. Others who don't understand you will persecute you. They will think that you are not a real believer. The job was persecuted by his friends. His friends kept irritating him every day. In this case, the lady also was being pestered by the roommate constantly asked her about getting tested if she is negative for the virus. She asked if now she is working after she saw her go out for a week. She even kept bothering her to see if she found a new accommodation to live in when there is still time to look. She invited her friend with her daughter to stay at the accommodation and overtake the fridge and freezer with their food leaving less than half the capacity for her to use. She told her that she will go to her country and bring her sister to come to stay with her in the room that the lady is renting. She emphasized again wanting her to move out even without her friend knowing that she messaged the lady to harass her. The lady ignores her messages being so annoyed by her. The Lord will punish our enemies.

Sadly, people, who mistreat a genuine believer though they claim to be a believer will also be punished. The roommate claimed that she is a real believer and said that she needs to teach a lesson, so the mistreatments and her showing by cooking food to give her to eat are being tested. She insisted that she wants to see the fruit in the lady and doesn't see it. All she saw was a child and kept looking with the eyes of flesh. She allowed the devil to use her by making her controlling, angry, doubtful, fearful, negative, judgmental, strict, and unamendable. She didn't want to support her inspired ideas that the Lord has given either. She refused to tell her friends. She insisted that she knows the Bible and must see the books before she can share them with friends. She judged based on what she observed and refused to reconsider. He will make one refuse to accept that believers can gain wealth and refuse the Holy Spirit.

If you read the Bible carefully, you will come to realize that the Lord only rebuked the love of money and selfish gain. All our forefathers were ordinary people that the Lord blessed and made into wealthy and rich people. He is not against wealth and riches, but only against the love of it and the love for the self to keep it. It was meant to bless others. The wicked of the world are enjoying wealth for their gain though they are creating solutions for people their motivation is for themselves. God uses the money to reach nations. Every vision He gives requires a huge amount of provision. People believe He doesn't need money, but on earth, certain things still require money transactions to be made. Without money, you can't do ministry and business unless a supernatural provision is granted.

One person said that this one has the fruit, but if she doesn't recognize a genuine believer that is led by the Holy Spirit there is great suffering to come. The devil knows that he has deceived the one who claims to be a believer. The Lord has promised that the innocent will also avenge. If you are persecuted within your household, the Lord will also avenge you and restore what you lost. People can be deceived and think that they know the Lord more than you, but it is by the Holy Spirit that one will know what kind of believer you are. The devil will use those who think that they are believers against the genuine believer to test and persecute them. The punishment on the one that persecutes is worse than the evil that they did.

The Lord Jesus Christ will give us a crown for each test that we successfully pass. He warned us not to be lukewarm. Know what the Bible says before you tell other people that they are wrong. We are accountable for what we tell others. People will not understand. The Lord has a time for everything. He will bring victory to those who are genuinely His. The lady has survived and passed through the Red Sea and has been parted as she has come

out of the sickness and gotten a new job. She was allowed to return
to her old job if she complies with the mandate of the organization
to be vaccinated. Coercion just for her to receive back what they
took away from her. They refused to compensate for the lost pay.
She knows life will get better as she leaves this accommodation. She
knows what she wants to be with other real believers to be free from
suffering. She is no longer under Pharaoh's control. Though this Pharaoh type is still trying to control her life but is failing yet she is still
irritating her. She has the victory even when the Pharoah type continually demands her to comply. She is faced with the person justi-
fying herself and accusing the lady. She kept persisting to move out
and then asked her questions about when she will move out. She is
bombarded with text messages while she is working.

The lady prayed with her prayer partner. She learned to ignore the
Pharaoh most of the time. Sometimes it was a challenge and she
gained wisdom from the Lord to respond. She endured the harass-
ment. She made a decision not to say anything except what the Lord
put in her heart and mind to say and write by messaging. She felt
the pressure that she had to find a place to move into. The owner of
the current place wanted to know when she will move out. When
she didn't have anyone confirmed to move her belongings, then
this owner wanted to provide a mover that is reasonably priced to
help. That mover agreed, but on the condition that the owner must
also help her to move all the belongings into the van. The lady was
warned that should she tell her this one will follow her to the new
place. That time the owner didn't mention that she will also assist to
unload the van at the new accommodation too. It is a danger for the
one who is against you to know where you will go next. They can
talk bad and also seek to get contact the new owner and may ruin
your reputation.

There was an accommodation recommended by a sister in Christ at
a condo downtown on the 23rd floor and if the lady is not employed
she can work part-time and use that to cover the other portion of the
rental cost. There was confirmation from the prayer partner that this

accommodation would not be beneficial for her. The lady didn't like downtown. She wanted a place in either the area she is staying in or the next district near it. The city is divided into districts. She found it would be more complicated if she lived downtown as her job and church at a bit north of the central district and also the church service is more east of her current location. Her job is further northwest.

The lady had to check with friends and her email to find out how to find new accommodation. It was already past the middle of February when she was rushing to find a new place to move. It was already February 11th. The Lord opened a door for a room for rent to be available and the room listing to be provided through an organization called Working Skills. She received the email listing on February 12th. A sister involved in the housing ministry provided information about accommodation. The lady checked the listing. She called the owner and arranged to meet him the next morning to visit the place. The weather that day that she called was too cold, so she was advised to come the next morning, and also she knew that it is on her way to church. It would be more convenient to go then. The arrangement was made to meet at the lobby first. The place is decent for the amount that it is rented. It gave her peace of mind to know from her prayer partner that she has almost obtained the new accommodation.

She met the owner before going to church service. The place for rent is a master bedroom with a half washroom that is private and a walk-in closet. A fridge, microwave, and veranda are included. It also has furniture indoor and outdoor to enjoy both environments. The owner of this place agreed to make a contract with her after her church worship service. The contract was signed and other agreements and receipts were made. A written copy was made and an electronic print-out copy was provided for both the owner and lady.

She met the owner of the accommodation that she would check into before going to church. He is nice and showed interest. He requested her to write down by dictation later the rental agreement and other details on paper and have it typed out. He and she would sign it after she came back from church. Her prayer partner confirmed that the arrangement is almost complete.

There was no proper rental agreement made at the other accommodation as there was no written agreement. The rules there were not set until issues began to arise. She questioned the owner at her current accommodation and told her that it would have helped. The owner/roommate agreed to pay her back one day of her last month's rent, the laundry card money, and her mail except any after February 28th. The lady told her to return the mail to the sender. The distance of travel is a bit far. The previous roommate was bothering her while she was at work. She had to ignore her.

The Lord has brought help to escape from the spirit of Pharaoh. Two men, the sons of the Lord's servant came to help move things out of where the lady lived. There was a bit of delay and some quarrels that occurred during the time of moving. The Lord protected us from accidents that almost happened. It took a few hours to move everything. The new owner was nice to treat the lady to dinner as he knew that she would be tired and she didn't have dinner. He also didn't have to help move her belongings. That was the agreement for him to relax based on his age being quite senior. The two men did most of the work in moving the belongings.

After the move was completed, she was able to start unpacking her belongings and the best decision about this move is that the following day is a holiday. It is Family Day and she was able to take the time to unpack more belongings and arrange her room more properly. The previous owner questioned the keys.

This is not the end of the suffering. The previous owner harassed the lady again while she was at work. She continued to accuse her of wrongdoing and refused to realize her sins. She started to teach the lady. The lady stopped her and made her realize that she didn't ask her to teach her, but only when the lady realized she needs to be taught. Then she will accept the teaching, but she never attended the bible studies that her roommate conducted and she also realized what kind of person that woman is. The woman still didn't recognize who the lady is.

When they met again, she told the lady that she didn't have to return her any money. She didn't stay until the agreed date of February 26/27th. The lady moved out by February 20th. She didn't know when she would move out of her current residence. She has to trust the Lord and speak prophetically though she didn't know that it would be earlier.

Chapter 5: New challenges

The new owner gave her a free week and more without paying rent for the rest of February. She only had to pay for the first month and last month's rent. This helped her to save a bit of finance from her current job.

She began to find difficulty in traveling to work and going back home. The travel time took about 3 days each day. She lost more time in waiting and traveling and worked more hours with less pay and time available. The company also required her to clock in and out. It stole time from her too. The lady was unaware that is not working immediately and is considered time fraud. The company only gave half an hour of lunch and restricted from accessing the phone more. She felt the pressure of rushing home and also trying to compete against the company time clock. Time was not well used sometimes. Evil also fights against us. He didn't allow her to return to the old job sooner. She has been waiting for it for at least two weeks, but still no response. A few times there were cautions and a warning that made her concerned that she might not be able to keep the job. She became doubtful at times. She longed to get out of the job and get back to the previous job. This also caused some slight hindrances on the job and some lecturing from her prayer partner.

The owner of the current accommodation that the lady moved to treat her so well as a queen. She received the spa treatment by getting a few bubble baths and having her hair repaired, moisturized, and puffed up. She was told again the next day. He was also feeding her a lot of food to make her gain weight. He shared his life stories and teach her about health and other things he knew including how to brush his hair using a special brush. Hair conditioning is only good for hairs that need restoration. Proper hair treatment will prevent hair loss too. It must be handled with care. He is into the practical aspects of life.

There is also a caution about people who seek to get close to you and do things for you. Favour is a great blessing, but some people need to be discerned for their motives in blessing you. It could be that they are trying to get you entangled with them. They want you to remain with them and not go anywhere else. This owner wanted to rent his place out to have somebody to stay connected with. He doesn't want to rent to any men and doesn't allow men to come even to visit unless it's his friends. He trusts the lady, but also really began to take great interest in her too. Some people say age doesn't matter, but there are certain times when it does matter. Where do you draw the line? If somebody is more than 20 years older, most people would agree this is too much of an age difference and considered unrealistic and can become creepy. If one doesn't have a boundary, they are in danger of allowing people to misunderstand. Once they see a boundary, they will have to retract though they may not always fully retract. A fox in character will always keep trying to pursue what he wants.

The Lord will protect us on the job, so even in the most challenging of times, we can keep our job. In some cases, the company may not be deserving of our contribution, so the Lord will close the door and open another door for us. We need to realize that when the Lord chose us we are not like the people of the world. Some believers have a peculiar anointing and calling that other people don't have. Everyone is unique, but not everyone is a one-of-a-kind person. These believers are rare but have gone through difficulties, and once they go through they are the most valuable in the eyes of the Lord and receive the greatest blessings, favour, and promotions. Others may not recognize them for who they are and what they have done. The only thing that matters is our relationship with the Lord.

Chapter 6: Tests

Finally, the lady received news on March 16th from the previous job because payroll contacted them. A pay statement was received at her apartment. She noticed it that same morning. She didn't realize at that time that the payment had been stopped. The HR manager spoke to her and favour was granted because she had signed a settlement agreement and was told she would get her job back. They had to grant her another job. She was informed that the job she was in was discontinued. That is the reason that they released it as a higher position that is permanent. There is one position open, but it is far for her in Etobicoke, so they will make arrangements to grant her another position closer to her home in Scarborough. She would not be going back to North York based on this. She would be contacted about it. She would be reinstated and would also be able to receive back all her benefits and compensation benefits and entitlements. She has to find another permanent job before this new temporary contract would expire.

A prophetic word was given to her a few weeks ago that she would have to wait until Easter time to get back to the previous company and get her pay raise. When she checked the date, it said April 17th. It is a month later. The current job mentioned that they would give a pay raise in April. April 18th may be the first day when she starts the new position near her home. She was doing warfare and prayers and expecting that she would get back in sooner than that.

The current job started to get busier on March 18th. Her sufferings are not yet over until the change of job is established. She has to endure taking the long ride to work and suffering loss of time and sleep and yet to be thankful to the Lord and remember the day of small beginnings. She must not despise it because when things get better, she may forget the suffering. The Lord will reward the sufferings we go through. He sees all that we do for Him in secret and will openly reward us. It may take time before it happens, do patience is required and constantly believing the Lord.

Christ suffered all things for us and He remembers it and reminds us of His sufferings. Paul suffered for the Lord's sake to share the gospel for the remaining days of his life. He had the freedom to some extent with restrictions, but he suffered much before he had an assigned permanent place to minister. Some people suffer for many years even 20 or more years in their situation before they see the victory and restoration. They have to hold onto the Lord daily to maintain their walk with Him and be always in prayer, worship, and the Word of God.

Stay in fellowship with other believers and pray, worship, and seek the Lord with them too. Maintain that daily. Prayer warriors are the best for spiritual warfare in times of suffering. Be strong in the Lord and His mighty power and forget not His benefits. Be like Joshua and remain serving the Lord no matter what you go through. Maintain a pure and holy walk and keep speaking the Word of God and not allow ourselves to speak ill words out of our mouths. There are small and large tests that we have to pass to excel in life. The Lord seeks those who are faithful to Him. Not everyone successfully endures difficulties in life for the Lord. There is a great reward for those who do.

One servant in the Lord suffered for at least 20 years and also lacked food and finances. The devil plays games using even the family, friends, and tenants to do evil. He will seek to destroy and keep you in a bind. He will do whatever He can to stop you from doing the ministry work of God even to change an aspect of your character. Are you able to maintain your integrity and a life of devotion to prayer almost 24 hours a day for so many years? You will go through sleepless nights and your body will become affected. You will be fasting if you are lacking food to eat. Your weight will be lost. Most people will experience stress. You will have lost a lot of finances over that period. The gathering of finances for the Lord was taken away for so many years by those who are against the Lord. People who think low of the Lord and don't realize that the Lord will judge one day mock. They despise and trample down on the servants of

God. The only comfort is the Lord and the servants of God through prayers, words, and support. A word of prophecy strengthens you in these sufferings. It will bring you out of your situation. The right time will come for the Lord to bring you out of it. The time of the Lord is always perfect. We must use the authority given to us.

Job was also tested and had gone through many difficulties before the Lord delivered him and restored him more than he had before. Job was faithful to the Lord and did not sin. He had to learn more about God, but the Lord still saw Job as a righteous man. He also rewarded him after he ended his suffering. Job was more blessed than before. He got back three daughters and more sons and livestock than before. He was wealthier than before and the Lord had given him a long life. His daughters were the most beautiful among the women.

Our heart attitude is tested and it is not easy to maintain when one suffers for a long time. There is also another who suffered at the hands of a narcissist for over 20 years and it is so traumatic and takes much healing to come out of the years of torment. One's reality can be greatly warped. Individuals can be so depressed and reject themselves and not believe anything about themselves. They experience worthlessness and always feel useless other than just surviving. This is the enemy's work to shake one's faith and to derail and cripple the individual, but nothing is impossible with the Lord. He can deliver and restore. One must rebuild their confidence in knowing their identity in the Lord and confess it daily until they are fully persuaded that it is their reality and then they will begin to transform and live out of that new reality.

The roots of bondage must be broken for healing to happen and then restoration. It takes time to restore, but the process will eventually increase in speed. As your heart becomes more receptive, you will receive a quickening of your spirit when you breakthrough through the cycles and are transformed. Freedom happens and it will become easier to seek the Lord in times of difficulty.

When a believer is feeling sick, they also need to break from the thought of the sickness and its symptoms, then they will have victory over it. The sickness or disease will leave them. Faith confession and taking authority in the name of Jesus Christ are crucial for healing to happen. It is also a requirement in dealing with attacks of the enemy against your life. You must fight spiritual warfare daily until a break-through happens.

The Lord can change a situation around completely as if it didn't happen. After 6 months, you can experience a different life that is abundant and prosperous. Nothing is impossible for the Lord. The Lord will send somebody to give you prophetic words to encourage you and give you what you need to bring you the strength to over-come. Trust the Lord that you will come out of the suffering. He is faithful and will bring us out. He will part the Red Sea and bring you to the promised land He has for you. You will cross the river of Jordan spiritually to receive the greater anointing. Do not despise the day of small beginnings. It is a reminder of what you have been through and where you began before success comes. Some have for-gotten their past and the Lord when they became successful in life. We must pray that we will not forget the Lord and those who were with us to help us. Remember the base foundation that the Lord chose to train you up. Stay honest, sincere, and humble. Show kind-ness and generosity and be thankful.

Joseph was in the prison for many years. People have said that it has been 13 years. He remembered the Lord and stayed close to the Lord all those years. The Lord gave him favour with the jailor and then he met the chief cupbearer and chief baker. The opportunity was given to interpret their dreams, but he was forgotten by the chief cupbearer and had to wait another two years before Pharoah had dreams and he got called out to interpret them. Joseph remembered the Lord and told Pharoah that it is God that gives the interpretation. He also gave Pharaoh counsel on what to do so he was promoted to the role of prime minister and given the best of the land that he needed . He was given abundance that same day. The Lord knows when we are ready to receive the promotion and abundance from Him. All of the old nature must be completely cut off. Our desire must be to glorify the Lord only. Then He will bless us with more than what we need. Joseph was so wealthy that he was able to provide more than enough for his family too. He sent caravans to get Jacob and the rest of the family members to come to Egypt to settle there. All your enemies will know that you are blessed. Joseph was known by all the people in the land. The Lord will also make you become known. He is a faithful steward and manager of finances and resources. He worked hard and set up the portion of payment for the people to return to Pharoah each year of their land and labour.

Jesus has the greatest suffering on the cross from the crown of thorns on his head, the nails that pierced his hands, and the spear that pierced his side. The pain of loss of blood and breathing and the weight of his body caused him to suffer more. The betrayal of disciples and his people. The shame and dishonour that He faced. The Lord Jesus Christ faced many tests and trials. The enemy was not able to defeat him. Jesus used the word of God to come against him. Learn from His life how he remained silent when he was questioned. The peace was with Him and the determination to endure the death on the cross for all humanity to be saved. Jesus also suffered thirst. Due to the hours, it took for them to crucify Him, there would be no food given. As we know, the last meal was the Last Supper with the disciples. We can learn more about this when we study the background of the crucifixion and the bible feasts. It is something that also needs to be discovered.

When we have overcome our sufferings, we count all for joy for the Lord. It is a great blessing to be counted worthy and experience suffering for Him in life. In the days ahead, there will be more suffering in the world. Are you ready to face the challenges that are to come? Will you remain faithful to the Lord in the days ahead? How much can you endure? Have you experienced financial loss? Have you been reduced to become small in people's eyes? Are your enemies mocking you and benefiting from the provisions you have worked hard to gather? Are you lacking sleep and your time is being wasted? Do you have cases against you? Are you being tested like Job or Joseph? Are you suffering for Christ?

An example of one in the Lord that has suffered in life, but also the promise of deliverance from their situation is found in Psalm 41:
1 Blessed is he that considereth the poor: the LORD will deliver him in time of trouble.
2 The LORD will preserve him, and keep him alive, and he shall be blessed upon the earth: and thou wilt not deliver him unto the will of his enemies.
3 The LORD will strengthen him upon the bed of languishing: thou wilt makes all his bed in his sickness.
4 I said, LORD, be merciful unto me: heal my soul; for I have sinned against thee.
5 Mine enemies speak evil of me, When shall he die, and his name perish?
6 And if he comes to see me, he speaketh vanity: his heart gathereth iniquity to itself; when he goeth abroad, he telleth it.
7 All that hate me whisper together against me: against me do they devise my hurt.
8 An evil disease, say they, cleaveth fast unto him: and now that he lieth he shall rise no more.
9 Yea, mine own familiar friend, in whom I trusted, which did eat of my bread, hath lifted up his heel against me.
10 But thou, O LORD, be merciful unto me, and raise me up, that I may requite them.
11 By this I know that thou favourest me, because mine enemy doth not triumph over me.
12 And as for me, thou upholdest me in mine integrity, and settest me before thy face for ever.
13 Blessed be the LORD God of Israel from everlasting, and to everlasting. Amen, and Amen.

The Lord told us that we will be tested and "The father shall be di vided against the son, and the son against the father; the mother against the daughter, and the daughter against the mother; the mother in law against her daughter in law, and the daughter in law against her mother in law (Luke 12:53)."

He told us to also be faithful to the end because He will reward us. There will be rewards in this life and also when we are in heaven. The apostles suffered for Christ and were considered worthy. Jesus Christ endured the suffering of the cross and all other forms of pain torture. He had great joy doing it because He knows that it will bring salvation to many. Some believers suffer persecution in worse ways and a number of them are known to us. Those who are faithful through suffering receive a great reward. They are given a crown for going through suffering.

The lady in this book lost 40 years of her life with the wrong people. She didn't learn the lessons she needed to learn and master in her 20s and became concerned about the things of the world. She didn't plan or develop a single career focus. She also is getting older in an age when it comes to marrying. Often men that don't have much became interested in her. She lost financially, relationally, and spiritually. She felt much guilt, shame, pain, and rejection too. She became angry, disappointed, sad, and despised her life. She needed to receive godly counsel and deliverance. She received that and began to have a turnaround in her life. It is a progression and takes time to recover and for life to become successful. She has to work at it. She took on a career change and pushed herself and spent time finding ways to increase her finances and utilize her skills. She sought ways to generate income.

Another issue came up which happened between her and the new owner. He was showing her compassion and sympathy, but began to like her and thought that he can develop a relationship with her and date her. He shared his past with her claiming that he is an honest man, but admitted that he has two girlfriends that he wants to dump because they didn't come to help him in his time of need. He has expectations of her as if she is his boyfriend. This man is being much older in age.

He has finances and properties and nobody he trusts to spend it on. He has tenants renting out his properties. He made his money by hiring women for his beauty salon and being a photographer among the rich and famous. The ex-wife and his son didn't speak to him. He has a daughter and a granddaughter that still connects with him and his rich friends. He invested in stocks and felt he can lure the ladies to like him, but never gave them money. He thought he can demand this lady to eat the food that he cooks that she didn't want. Most of the time he made food that she was willing to eat. He treated her like a queen. When he thought to consider her as a tenant, he set a strict time for cooking and for washing. He tempted her with things she would like and want. The Lord showed he is a fox and a womanizer.

A man who likes to be around the rich, but is a poor man is a dishonest person. He learned to work hard and generate income and become rich. He claimed that he is a Christian but is religious and by the way, he lives his life he proved that he has not encountered the Lord in his life. He gets in conflict and swears when he is angry with telemarketers that call his home line. He has a temper that he showed when he couldn't get what he wanted. He also has cheated and still cheating on the taxes. He only allowed the rent to be claimed excluding the utilities, laundry, and Internet charges that he charged extra. The arrangement for rent was by mouth which he requested to be typed out and was not a legal agreement. Eventually, the Lord will punish that person when he comes against the servant of the Lord.

Chapter 7: Sexual Bondage

There are people that the devil will send to stir up doubt in you so that you won't trust the Lord and the Lord's servants. Be aware of those who appear to be godly. The enemy tempts us in our time of weakness and brokenness. In a time of relational suffering, one can be tempted to leave the very person that the Lord has given to us. He will cause division, strife, and anger. He can also cause somebody who is not born-again and the spirit-filled believer to commit sexual sin with another. It can be a person in the Lord also. That bondage that gets formed will cause deception to form and the two will believe that they are still okay. They dont' understand the consequences of the sin nor its effects.

Unfortunately, it corrupts the person's spiritual walk with the Lord. It will keep them bound and they will lose out on blessings. They don't realize there is a curse also. If they are serving in the church, they will be removed from serving. This is considered contamination. It leads to a life of rebellion and attack from the enemy. The person will suffer in their life. Their connection with God is also affected, so the anointing and flow that operated are withheld. They may not be sound in their thinking and actions. They will be led astray and also don't feel God. They begin to lose their desire for the Lord. They will be hindered from praying, worshipping God, and reading the Bible. They won't be able to hear the Lord clearly. People also look down on the person. They feel not loved and the worst decision is to isolate themselves from the church. They lose their love for the Lord. They are focused on worldly things and have the gap filled.

A Jezebel type and narcissist can also cause sexual sin. It makes the person's life and prayers ineffective and unproductive. Only when the person truly repents and comes out of the sin and cuts off the ties with the other person, they will experience freedom and restoration. The person has to totally cut that person from their life. Then they will become spiritually strong again. Sexual sin also changes the countenance of a person. One pastor that committed this had a very strong stinky odour that only could be smelled by somebody who has the gift to smell the odour. The Lord has taught some servants of God how to deliver people from sexual sin and other bondages.

There is a ministry that teaches how to break free from sexual bondage and sin with detailed prayers covering all aspects and evil spirits as well as principalities. We are also responsible to maintain our deliverance after it has ministered. Sometimes we still experience pain and shame. We need to renew our minds and believe what the Word of God tells us that we are forgiven and free. We are a new creation in Christ Jesus. He has purchased us by His blood. He has cleansed us and given us a new life. We are the head and not the tail. We are victorious through Christ Jesus. We are an overcomer and more than a conqueror. He transforms us day by day. We need to know our identity in Christ when we are battling with our past and remind the devil that he is defeated. We have to cast down every thought and make it obedient to Christ Jesus. We need to know that every weapon formed against us will not prosper. We need a new picture of who we are in Christ. Jesus Christ can give us a vision if we ask Him to replace the past. You can receive the healing. Remember it is the devil that reminds us of our past and gives us a defeated mindset. He puts fear in our hearts. He seeks to kill, steal, and destroy. We must be bold and keep him under our feet. Use your authority in the name of Jesus against his plans and any evil spirits that come against you.

Rejection is one of the root causes for sexual sin. Guilt, shame, and condemnation also are other reasons. Satan attacks these people in childhood and it can be while they are in the womb. He can put fear and a lack of trust in authority. Once the individual forms these mindsets and rebellion, they will be driven by them. Repentance, deliverance, and your commitment to obey the Lord are the solutions. You need a spiritual counselor that knows how to deal with the root of the problem. This bondage also passes through generations. Once it is cut from the individual forever, they will need to take caution in training their children in the ways of the Lord and make them aware of his vulnerability. They must pray for God's protection daily.

Chapter 8: Financial struggles

The lady that was first mentioned also had to go through other financial difficulties including scammers and greed. People can recommend you to invest in cryptocurrency but if you aren't monitoring it then you will lose what you gained and most of your investment too. These days scammers are getting wiser about how they can deceive individuals. The most recent scam that this woman experienced is somebody pretending to call from Amazon with an actual prerecorded message regarding identity theft. There is a representative on the line waiting for you to press '1" and once you connect they will tell you that somebody had created an account with your name and linked 7-8 bank accounts. They tried to purchase a Macbook Pro and Apple earbuds. If you verify that this is false, they will request details. Then they will connect you to another individual that pretends to be the assistant to the Crown Attorney General.

They provided a legitimate address and the phone number and the name of the person that works in this position. They will also verify your information and write you a letter after they claim to go to court. The person told her to wait on the phone line. The person asked her to provide the names of the banks you are a client with and the types of accounts plus the balances without asking for bank account numbers and bank card numbers. They will require that you don't call the bank, or others, or communicate with the police. They will also tell you to lie to the bank owner and save their phone number into your phone under the title as somebody very important like a spouse and to say it's for personal use.

These days people can create an account to make it legitimate to send money to and request you to purchase Bitcoin through an Instacoin machine. This method is hard to track and the company that owns it will not refund your money especially if you get scammed. They know how to use system-generated phone numbers to maintain confidentiality and use a few at a time. When they are caught, they will block and discontinue the numbers.

When she prayed to the Lord and spoke to one of the credit card companies, they reversed the charges on her card. The bank reversed the charges that were made and restored the cash that was withdrawn. A police report had to be completed. The scammers also had made a call to threaten her arrest. She called the police again and was told they can't arrest her. She was advised to block all their numbers.

There are countries that are more knowledgeable about catching scammers. They know how to utilize technology to help locate them. Every scam has a root to it. The root cause is usually greed and victimization. It also can be from a cheating spirit and deception

As believers when we are alone and have been through various situations and stress, we are not at our best and will not be able to discern the situation and people around us. This lady had also been through other situations in and out of the church. We can make bad decisions when we fail to plan for the future and to receive God's counsel and follow His instructions. We will experience much financial loss.

The Lord can restore back the finances that the devil steals from us. We can take authority and demand for it to be returned back to us. We can request for Jesus to take it back from the devil on our behalf. There are ministers that will tell you to go before the courtroom of God to plead before Him to demand this. The Lord will judge the devil for you. We will get back seven times more when we demand the return back from him to be a hundredfold and seven times more.

If you have not been tithing, it is important that you start to tithe because it is your protection over the finances against the enemy. Ministers will tell you to pay 10% and give 10%. You should have 10% savings and 10% investments. You should have another 10% for emergencies, and the remaining balance is for spending.

For those who are students, it is a good practice to save aside money while you are studying. If you can manage a part-time job or sum mer employment, you should apply the financial principles of the scriptures into practice to plan for your future. It is wise to plan earlier in life. Some believers suffered much in life for not being good stewards in their youth. Family and friends will only support you up to a certain extent. The rest is your hard work and obedience to the Lord that will prosper you. Some believers plan well and become prosperous in life.

The Lord gave them wisdom and ideas and they believed and obeyed the instructions. Some become rich but sometimes they face difficulties in relationships when they are entangled with the wrong people. Make sure you receive confirmation from the Lord when you pray to ask what to do in every aspect of your life. This will save you from suffering from the wrong decisions you make. Avoid overspending and buying what you don't need. Make sure you have an RRSP and contribute to it regularly and yearly. It's good to have a GIC and savings account. There are others that invest in stocks or cryptocurrency which has its risks. Bonds are good too. You can consider stable investments or those with better results and more risks. People also purchase land, gold, and silver if possible.

Be careful about the spirit of greedy as it can bind you into snares. The devil doesn't want Christians to be prosperous. He can bring people to make your life suffer and cause you to be robbed financially. In some cases, he can put court cases against people. He knows how to keep people in a bind for several years. He can keep stealing and oppressing until the Lord delivers you out. You need to consult him all the time how to overcome and change the situation in your faovur.

When you have debt, you should pay it off as soon as possible and cut back on unnecessary expenses. Others will tell you to also get another job or generate income which there are various ways you can achieve this.

In the body of Christ, we also can face individuals that are cheaters and greedy for money. They make promises that they don't keep or persuade you so that they can gain. Learn to discern people's hearts and not to trust people with money unless the Holy Spirit leads you who to give to and how much. Money exposes a person's heart. Most people will become full of greed when they have abundance and they will abuse and persecute others. Satan uses the same tactics to deceive us as he deceived Eve. He will always present us a good opportunity which is not the best. He will use believers and those who claim to be Christians. They will have other motives or they may seem to good people but there is some issues in their lives.

Satan uses the same tactics to deceive us as he deceived Eve. He will always present us with a good opportunity that is not the best. He will use believers and those who claim to be Christians. They will have other motives or they may seem to be good people but there are some issues in their lives.

There is a case where an elderly prayed for a tenant and her friend knows a lady looking for accommodation. The lady was not planning to move yet and was busy preparing to travel the next morning. She was pressured for time. The devil uses the worst time to trap us so that we make errors. She decided to visit the place since the sister in Christ persuaded her to take a look. She felt the pressure to check it out without praying about it to reconsider whether it is ideal for her schedule. She made it clear that she is busy and didn't much that much time. She came to visit the place and thought about it. Her concern is to have accommodation to move to for September and not for August. It was late July when she visited this place. She made it clear to the friend that she would be away for a month. The owner wanted to rent the room for cash. She said that she has some walking difficulty. She needs support and it's not convenient for her to visit the bank without assistance. She is a nice lady and very supportive. She had no receipt book to write a receipt but only a word of promise. She wanted the first and last month's rent. The three of them are a witness in this situation. The lady was never told that the elderly

owner has any health issues. She left expecting that things would
be fine and that she would have peace of mind moving after over a
month.

Another individual renting contacted her about a place she liked
more and wanted to consider that and take back her rental deposit
and informed the friend to let the owner know. The owner's daughter
became involved and found out and said that they would be willing
to do that for her upon her return but did not tell her any further details.

Unfortunately, when the lady returned from her visit home to collect
her money back the owner was acting in disarray. The daughter said
that the mother has dementia yet she admitted to having collected the
rent money from her. There was no other evidence showing a signa
ture and name signing to that arrangement other than the verbala-
greement and the friend being witness to the transaction. It didn't
work in favour of the lady. These people also said that they cannot
reimburse the funds unless they can find them. This woman is short
of funds also. The owner, later on, disclosed that she had used the
money to pay her taxes. The children said that she had no money in
her hands and didn't deposit so somebody is lying. The owner also
thought that somebody may have come to her home to use her washroom and taken it. Another thought before is she may have put it in
a plastic bag and accidentally threw the bag in the trash. The Lord
knows and sees all things. People who do not pay back to us will get
problems to happen to them. The Bible is clear that we reap what we
sow both good and bad.

Once a deposit is made at another place, the money is difficult to retrieve back. It is considered an agreement unless they are willing to
return it. Though this owner is nice there is an issue with her as later
on the children said she has dementia. Our confession of our words
matters in our decisions in life and how we perceive others and situations. The only options people generally will tell you is to report to
the police to have them resolve the case and find out what happened.

When there is a lack of documentation, it is not beneficial for the victim. Inseeking the Lord, ministers will recommend coming before the courtroom of God to make a request for the Lord to judge your case and demand on the devil to return the money back and pay the seven times. Jesus has to take it back from him. If we have sinned, we must repent before the Lord can intervene on our behalf. Make sure you have no unforgiveness holding against the person or any other offences. Hatred, bitternes, anger, and revenge should not be in our heart. It will hinder our prayers being answered. Satan is a legalist. He will use anything that is sinful against us. We must have a clean conscience. Then the Lord will bring back all the finances and more to us and we must be patient to wait for it.

In this situation of the lady, she has been advised to confront the woman and instill the fear into her that she must obtain the rent back from the woman. She had to take authority over this situation and command forth a tenant to be connected to the owner to pay her rent and the lady has to make sure that she collects the rental money from this owner. At the same time, she must be wise because of the children's connection. The children are not cooperating.

The Lord will grant the financial breakthrough but it will take time to receive the results after following the instructions that He gives you. The Lord will give us ideas and ways to increase but we must remember to put Him and the Kingdom first. He will allow us to use a portion of the finances for our needs too.

We need to be careful about the friends that we have in our lives. People who are not focused on planning for the future and are good at money management are not suitable friends. Some believers are also suffering from bad decisions made from their youth onward.

Some parents try to educate their children but the children don't realize the importance of what they are being taught. They will discover it later in age and feel the hardship in life. They are considered late bloomers. They take more time to mature and become independent and wiser about their decisions. Individuals that have been victims of abuse tend to have difficulty with life's decisions. They make more mistakes and get entangled in bad relationships that keep them bound financially too. They find themselves in debt also either from their own decisions or because of the relationship they are in. Some narcissists tend to have financial problems. They have debts caused by their own decisions. They are entangled in multiple relationships and the one who married them will also suffer financially. They tend to exceed the speeding limit when they drive or break other driving or parking regulations too. They tend to be unrealistic. Some also get into legal cases through tenancy agreements or relationships. If you are a victim of these kinds of people, you must get help and leave the relationship quickly. It is the best decision for your life. The amount of trauma one can experience will cripple the person. Mentally they cannot function normally so if they can be deceived by people financially they may not be able to discern until it's too late.

If you are an author but aren't able to spend much to market your books, you will have to spread it by word of mouth, social media, family, friends, and church. As an author, it has been a challenge to market books. People are in the membership without having to purchase to pay for the book individually. These days they don't have to pay for your book to read it which really is a disadvantage for the author who is expecting royalties. Overspending also must be cut from our lives. Be wise to budget your spending. Avoid debt and money-rich scams. Avoid network marketing opportunities as they are considered scams and you will lose friends and have conflicts. When you have money, people come to you and when you don't they will leave you. Be aware of those who come to you when you have rich.

The lady also tried to market the books that she wrote without spend
ing more on promotion. She tried paying individuals to market her
books but the success rate was low. She found that she didn't have as
many results and was better off promoting her books. She was given
offers to promote her books and the costs are high for her budget.
She tried to set up her website to promote her teaching series with
limitations. There is much more required to make a website function
successfully to generate sales. She invested also in a stock portfo-
lio that was doing well until a decline happened and she lost 11% of
her investment. She wants to get a home of her own but she is short
on the deposit for a down payment and short on pensions and retire-
ment savings. She also didn't have her driver's license and decided
to focus on her career. Her friend called her a late bloomer. She had
to pay for her part-time studies as her job refused to grant her tuition
reimbursement even though they have that fund. She needed to have
a job related to her studies to cover the costs. She felt a lot of financial strain. She had been cheated by several people in different ways
and she had to learn to manage and plan how she should properly
manage her finances. She had been easily deceived into fraud and
had to cut that tie from her life too. She didn't have much financial
help from others. She tried to get another job in additional to her current job and found it challenging.

She had to continually seek the Lord and work with whatever the
Lord gave her. She managed to set aside finances for her part-time
studies and work full-time. She was encouraged that she will have a
better job after she completes her studies. She would have to be patience to transition into the career and have a better job and life. Remember in all life circumstances the Lord will deliver us. It will be
on His time and His way. We have the authority to change situations
and to pray for things to be accomplished in our life sooner. In the
later days, we will need to really trust the Lord for His provision.

There is a case where an individual had fallen into fraud. They invested their finances into a trading platform that does currency and cryptocurrency as well as stock exchanges. They buy and sell from genuine places but the organization is a deception. They lure the individual into investing a basic standard of $250 in USD to their credit card. The transaction will show some other name. When you check into it, you will see it's a website that could be related to learning about trading. An example is Intel Academy does have this $250 investment requirement for accessing their program. The trading company agent has also falsified their advertising through YouTube pretending that they are working with Elon Musk for Quantum AI technology. There is a website but you will find that it is a registration-only website and there is further access.

Once you have decided to complete the form, somebody with an international number will contact you. If you take the call, they will confirm that they work with Quantum AI but will transfer you to another agent. This individual will be persuasive and nice to speak with. They will request to go through all the procedures required of a standard trading company. They created an account for you after they received your funds before the call and they will show you that they have invested and it is successful.

You will find out from them their company is called GetPrime Crypto. They have a website. Some articles mention it's a scam. Sadly, they are on BHVN with the registered number 96960, Ajeltske Island, Majuro, Republic of the Marshall Islands MH according to the website. You will notice on the contact page that it says Sweetwood Drive Street, Boulder, Colorado 80302. The number says +44-1568605271 and you can contact them on Whatsapp. It is getprimecrypto.net. People have complained that they are hard to catch and they should be caught. They have gained much wealth from people. The agents all have the title of the financial advisor. They also have mentors and they have teams of staff doing this trading. You may sometimes hear the other staff on the phone in the background. The email also looks legitimate and has a contact allocated to it. They usually maintain the scheduled time that you book them. They tend to work long hours and the standard Monday to Friday but their time zone is another country. They like to go after Americans and Canadians. Sometimes they use Manitoba or otherwise, it's the UK and other foreign numbers.

The method they use is AnyDesk or TeamViewer program that allows computers to be connected and they can access while you are using the computer at the same time. They cooperate with you to convince you that you can trust them as legitimate. If you choose to invest further with them, then they will ask you about your financial goals and the banks that you invest in. The idea is to create a plan for you to grow your finances. They can manage the account for you. You do gain profit from the investment and they give you bonus deposits when you invest more into the company. They exchange your money for Bitcoin to transfer it to their crypto wallet and will add the balance to your account. You will see it growing. They teach you how to use the platform. They ensure that you fully trust them with your money. They gently persuade you to invest more funds to get your account to grow quickly from basic to silver. The goal is to get you to platinum status. They will give you a copy of the document showing the goal they have for you but tell you not to share it with anyone. They have a different crypto wallet for transactions. They make sure that it's not as easy to track. They ask you to show them your bank accounts while you are on the computer.

They guide you and this is so they know how much investment potential you have. They will persuade you to also withdraw funds from GICs, RRPS, TFSAs, Mutual Funds, High-Interest savings, etc to make sure they get as much money from you.

They make sure you have Ndax to do e-transfers or wire transfers from your bank to your Exodus wallet. They use the Exodus wallet for transferring from crypto over to their account. There is a great gain opportunity but the deception however is not always realized that soon.

They will eventually assign another agent who is more aggressive to push you even harder to invest more and borrow from your credit card or line of credit to invest in their event. They can also borrow money from their own company to use for investment. They will require you to pay in a few days. If you request them to use the profit gained from the investment, they will insist that you must pay the borrowed balance before the profit is released to you. They will pursue you. If you have caught on by this point, you will choose to ignore their calls and they will keep trying until they decide to email you that they may take legal action against you. This is as far as most scammers go. The individual lost most of their hard-earned income to this scam.

Police will tell you that they cannot come against you. They will tell you because it's an overseas scam they don't have the resources to catch these people. They are capable to change their phone numbers by using apps. Computers also is another matter. They may have a limit or many depending on how much funds they were able to collect from people. They will also know when you request a withdrawal of your funds and will deny releasing it to you. They will go to the extent of either locking your access or making sure that your account becomes bankrupt so that you have no finances remaining in the account that they created for you. They make sure not to return your finances. If you contact these places that are involved in the process they will advise you to report to the police, banks, the fraud website, and crypto fraud people, and that is as far as it goes. You must go to the extent to change your phone number because this trading company will call you with various long-distance unknown numbers. They will call more than three times a day. They will never leave a voice message even if you do get voice messages they will have no voice recorded in them.

Unfortunately, the banks will not refund you the funds even when you tell them that you suffered fraud. They have disclosed ahead of time when removing the funds from your investments or even through the line of credit that you need to be careful and that if it is fraud they will not reimburse your loss. All cryptocurrency exchanges and wallets will inform you that they cannot reverse any transactions made. They cannot trace the culprit. Your only solution is the Lord. Then the Lord will restore us as we repent for our unwise decision and demand that the devil must repay us 7x more for what he stole from us. The Lord will restore it when we have faith to believe for this miracle to happen then we will have it. It takes time to receive miracles from the Lord. We may not always be patient enough to wait for His perfect timing. He knows when to release us. Otherwise, our flesh gets in the way and will rob us again of the blessings. God adds to us and the burden is always light. If you feel pressured by anyone or that the opportunity to too good, it is highly possible that it's a scam. Fear and worry usually come either during the process of the scam or after when it's completed. If you have more awareness sooner, you will know it.

The Lord can do impossible miracles but it will not be the way scammers do it. You will have peace when it is from the Lord. Always get confirmation from the Lord before you proceed. Start small and avoid investing big unless it's a regulated and trustworthy source. Cryptocurrency investment isn't the issue. It is the scammers that are utilizing technology to deceive people to invest in their wallets so that they can't retrieve it back. The Lord Jesus Christ is our Advocate against the devil. We can demand the judgment of the Lord against him. The Lord will give you wisdom and the root issues to deal with situations and cycles in your life.

Perhaps, this was mentioned before greed is the root problem for fraud, and the other is being too preoccupied with many responsibilities or tasks. When we don't spend time with the Lord and we are alone, we are in danger of being deceived. Scammers will call whatever numbers they can gather from the Internet. They have ways to get your phone number even if you are on the Do not call list. There is somebody that said that they don't get scam calls. This is very rare. Most people do and they usually ignore it but others are victims of scammers. Even corporations can be deceived if they are not careful to pay attention to details and do their research. Lawyers that specialize in fraud might or may not be able to assist in these matters.

The devil also can use his agents of destruction to put a court case against you. All the finances or properties that you have to gather require the Lord's protection. The devil can utilize people to steal it from you so that you suffer. He can prolong the suffering for several years and keep you in a cycle. Be aware of any covenants that you have previously made. The devil is a legalist. He will utilize your vows against you and any legal rights of access that he has over you. Any open doors you have given for him to access will keep you bound until you break them.

Deliverance is the only way and prayers for spiritual warfare will break these cycles. Avoid making promises that involve confession of poverty and hunger for yourself. It is not biblical. Jesus is all about faith confession. We must always have more than what we need so that we can be a blessing to others. Some sufferings are due to personal sins. We must know from the Lord which ones are from our own decisions versus the devil. God has all the solutions to provide you with the objections required to win your case. He can teach you how to become an advocate amid your suffering. He can show you the visions, ideas, and solutions required. He will tell you the outcome of the court cases. He will also inform you what is the cause of your sufferings and what are your sins. He can still provide for you through others during your time of suffering. Some people starve since they have limited resources and regularly fast and pray. The Lord will give us counsel directly and through others and dreams. You must wage good warfare to win.

Your own family can be your worst enemy when the devil is working. These individuals have all the characteristics of how the devil works and acts. They are users, abusers, narcissists, liars, hypocrites, fraudsters, greedy, utilizing their wisdom for your loss, starvation, destruction, etc. That also includes your death and that they gain everything that you possess. They will not use their own money but will take all of yours and enjoy it without any thought for the future and God's kingdom. They do the devil's work and their selfish desires. Make sure you have a committed team of leaders, prayer warriors, and intercessors on your side but you also must do the warfare daily and probably 24 hours and maybe 7 days a week until the Lord delivers you. You must always consult the Lord for instructions and if there are any blockages you need to break and deal with them. This includes unforgiveness. If you promised the Lord and didn't do it, then you need to complete it or ask forgiveness and renounce it. When it comes to tithing, you must release it to the Lord as soon as possible. Do not delay this because it is what protects the rest of your finances.

The Lord will open doors of opportunity for us. We need to pray and wait on the Lord to find out and get confirmation before we involve in financial decisions that have risks. Then we will recognize the right opportunities. There are blessings that we are unaware of until the Lord connects us to the right people to bring that blessings to us. If you have been scammed, you might not know when the right opportunity comes. You may be tempted to dismiss it because of previous experiences with scams or counterfeits.

Conclusion

As human beings, we are prone to weaknesses. We see the world as we believe it so our minds are limited by our mentalities. When we yield ourselves to the Lord, then transformation and conformation can manifest. We tend to choose for ourselves what we believe is best for us. We often forget the Lord when we are overwhelmed with the cares of life. Too often we forgot the promises and the scriptures. The Lord wants us to be like Mary and not like Martha. Too many believers or Christians are occupied with the things of this world and its issues. The devil uses the world and people in our atmosphere to distract, detour, and derail us from our calling. The Lord explicitly reminded us in the scripture that we must guard our hearts and be aware of the words that we speak. We must be careful and take advantage of every opportunity presented before us. Every second of our lives matters and it is counted.

The Lord knows how much time we spend with Him and doing what we have been destined to do. We are so fixated on the world's demands on our lives that we cannot concentrate. We have to go back to the Bible just to find consultation and consolation for our problems. We have to be determined to sit in silence away from all the distractions and hindrances just so that we can reflect and seek the Lord's face. Then we receive counsel and solutions. The Lord will provide the solution for us if we diligently seek Him. Jesus commended Mary for choosing the better choice. She laid all her matters before the Lord and just sat at His feet to listen to the teachings and apply them. She has faith and trusts that all things will be taken care of. She received strength, wisdom, and all that she required to approach her day. She rested and was at peace. Martha was always preoccupied with responsibilities and chores. She was distracted and unable to enjoy her life. She was constantly overwhelmed and seeking ways to resolve her issues on her strength. She even demanded for Jesus get Mary to help her. Jesus is so loving and understanding towards us, but He also gently reminds and corrects us. He knows that without Him we are not able to handle the matters in our life. Every problem has a solution in the Lord but not everyone wants to come to Jesus for the solution. Man naturally assumes that they can do it on their strength. We suffer for the unwise decisions that we make.

In this world, there will always be temptations and trials. We need to be strong in our walk with the Lord to maintain our faith, especially in the days to come that will be more intense than they are present. The Lord has given us time to gather and be wise to utilize all that we can before the conditions in the world worsen. We need to be prepared with extra resources and all that is required. Follow the Holy Spirit's direction every day. We will also need to learn how to walk in the supernatural power of God as Jesus did. There may come a time when there is scarcity and shortages. We have been warned about banks will eventually fail and cryptocurrency scams have increased but this is also the new currency that experts are focused on and many rich people and the working class have been seeking and investing to grow especially during the pandemic. At the same time, be wise about where you invest. We have been warned that stocks are dropping in and fluctuating also. It used to have great growth potential before the pandemic happened and now things are pending on how the market and economy recovers in the years to come. It has become uncertain when it will rise again.

Be attentive to the events happening in how they align with the scriptures, discern and know the times we are in, and save for the future. Gold, silver, and land are still valuable when things change. Prepare for emergencies. Be careful about social media and communication channels in what you share with others.

In these last days, our relationship with the Lord and hearing His voice will be what saves us from the evil to come.

Salvation Prayer

God, I know that I have sinned against you. Forgive me for the wrong that I have done. I believe that Jesus Christ died on the cross for me and that He was became rose from the grave. That I can have His eternal life. Come into my heart to be my Lord and Savior. I choose to turn away from my sins and to follow you. Lead me to walk with you. Keep me safe and teach me your ways. I cancel every plan of the enemy against my life. I renounce every covenant that I have made. I take authority in Jesus' name to close every open door in my life. Holy Spirit fill me now in Jesus' name. Amen.

Baptism in the Holy Spirit

Jesus you are the one that fills me with Your Holy Spirit. Come Holy Spirit and come into my life and fill me to overflow with Your presence. Come with your fire too. Thank you for the gift of tongues and your anointing in Jesus' name. Amen.

Open your mouth and let the words come out that God gives you. It will be words that you don't know what they mean. God can give you the meaning when you ask Him. Keep giving God your mouth to speak it out. You need to let Him talk through you every day to grow this gift. He will also take you closer to God and you will know more about Jesus and have power from God to do great things and know things.

Prayer

Father God, thank you for Jesus Christ sacrifice that brought me freedom. Give me the strength and the joy to go through tests, trials, and temptations. That I would also be able to endure sufferings for you. I pray for boldness and an overcoming spirit. That my life would bring you glory in everything that I do. Protect me from evil, deception and speaking negative words out of my mouth. Protect everything that belongs to me. Grant me discernment to know who you have assigned for my life and to guard me from the wrong people in Jesus name. Amen.

Message from the Author

This was an inspired idea by my prayer partner and co-warrior to share experiences about suffering for Christ. Believers are supposed to be victorious but it doesn't mean that we won't have difficulties in our lives. There is still going to be persecution and suffering as Jesus Christ told us. It is how we handle them and who we hold onto that brings us success. Most of the experiences in this book may not be great suffering to many but it is difficult for the individual that is living through them. God has given grace in different measures to each one depending on the situations that they experience in their lives. We are trained for our calling. The Lord will not allow us to face challenges that are too difficult for us and He will always make a way out of temptations. We need to restrain our flesh in difficult times. We must always have an accountability partner to connect with that will pray with us and for us. They should be there to guide us to walk with the Lord and correct us. I pray that you will draw closer to the Lord and experience breakthroughs and joy. That you would experience the blessings and favour of God and endure the sufferings for His glory.

Other Products

The Bridal Collection
Knowing God
How to Hear God's Voice
New Life in Jesus
Loving Israel
God's Gifts
Meeting God
Word Power
Fruit of the Spirit
The Tabernacle
Bride for Jesus
A Life of Prayer
Live Free
Who am I in Jesus
Walk in Love
God's Favor
Man of God
Woman of God
How to Use Money
God's Wisdom
Fasting
See Jerusalem and Bethany
First Fruit Offering
Pentecost
Feast of Trumpets
Day of Atonement
Feast of Tabernacles
Counting the Omer
Festival of Lights
Glory, Presence, and Holy Spirit
Live in God's Presence

31 Day Devotionasl
Biblical Puzzle Book Vol 1
Biblical Puzzle Book Vol 2
Biblical Puzzle Book Vol 3
Biblical Puzzle Book Vol 4
Biblical Puzzle Book Vol 5
Bible Puzzles for Young Children Book 1
Bible Puzzles for Young Children Book 2
Bible Puzzles for Young Children Book 3
Biblical Puzzles for Children Book 1
Biblical Puzzles for Children Book 2
Biblical Puzzles for Children Book 3
Smokey the Cat

Teaching Series & Guides
How to Hear God's Voice Teaching Guide
Knowing God, Jesus, and Holy Spirit
Relationship with God, Jesus, Holy Spirit Guide
Flowing in the Prophetic

And much more!

Please check Chelsea's website for links to other books and products found onAmazon, Barnes and Noble, and Kobo. Please leave a review to help the author to write more books.

https://chelseak532002550.wordpress.com

YouTube channel:
https://www.youtube.com/channel/UCOvw9wUmkE08Akeq2z3TQVA

Chelsea Kong Biography

She is a writer, creative arts and digital media artist, and skilled administrative professional. She graduated from Hotel and Restaurant Management, Digital Media Arts, Office Administration, and is studying to become a Payroll Practictioner. She also served in a variety of roles from audio visual, photography, to assisting on the worship team, and ministry team. She is also has a passion for families being united. Her writing consists of children books, stories, bridal writing, poems, lyrics for songs, word of encouragement, blessings, prayers, and jokes. She is the author of the Bridal Collection, Knowing God, How to Hear God's Voice, New Life in Jesus, Loving Israel, God's Gifts, Meeting God, Word Power, Fruit of the Spirit, The Tabernacle, Bride for Jesus, A Life of Prayer, and etc. She is also has her own Bible Puzzle books and other inspired products. These books teach children principles about faith and Christian life. She also has her own 31 days devotional, audiobook, teaching series on How to Hear God's Voice, Relationship series, and other inspired products. She is an organizer and tour guide for Favor Tour Ministries. Her podcast channel on self-development called Chelsea K on Anchor, Spotify, iTunes, and etc. Her podcasts can also be found on YouTube. She was interviewed on TheLadyTraceyShow on Unity-Live Radio. She has an article published in the Readers Magnet and highly recommended by A Proud Christian blog.

www.ingramcontent.com/pod-product-compliance
Lightning Source LLC
Chambersburg PA
CBHW080333030726
47593CB00010B/2986

* 9 7 8 1 9 9 0 3 9 9 1 7 6 *